Introduction to
Magick

?

FOCUS
your attention on your desire

PRACTICE
feeling what it feels like
to get what you want

DON'T GIVE A FUCK
about the outcome

Magickal Process

Introduction

The word magick was put into use by Aleister Crowley, who wanted to differentiate between stage magic and spiritual/metaphysical magick. This workbook explores what magick is and how to use it.

Magick is the cultivating of personal power–the remembering of our inherent divinity. We all have the ability to create the reality of our dreams, and using magick is a fun method for working with universal laws to create intended outcomes.

Sometimes, magick is just listening for answers from the nonphysical. *The Talking Board* exercise is perfect for accessing the wisdom already inside of you.

Spellcasting is another aspect of magick. When you focus your attention on what you want using rituals, crystals, potions, and altars, you create a powerful signal that reflects back to you in the form of manifestations. *The Cauldron*, *Ritual Altar*, *Talisman*, *Vision Board* and *Sigil Magick* all work with your focused intention. They help you project what you want to receive back.

But don't you just wish you had a magick wand to grant your every wish? Then the first exercise in this book is for you–using your problems to harness energy, transmute what is not wanted into exactly what *is* wanted with the flick of your wrist.

Meditation on How to Practice Your Magick

Breathe in and raise your vibration!
Breathe out and release your resistance.

Breathe in and raise your vibration!
Breathe out and release your resistance.

Relax. Say thank you for everything that's around you right now. The air you breathe, the water you drink, the food you eat, the floor that's holding you up, the sun that's shining.

Breathe in and be here now.
Breathe out and let your thoughts go.

Only your thoughts can make you feel bad. You can choose to step into the present moment right now.

Breathe in and be here now.
Breathe out and feel better already.

Listen to the flow. You get to choose what you feel and what you think. You are free to be whoever you want to be. Allow yourself to let go of everything else but what's in the present moment. Allow yourself to wake up in the dream right now.

Breathe in and smile!
Breathe out and decide how you want to feel.

Life is bringing you gifts in every moment. What you want is being handed to you right now. You can relax and enter the present moment, where everything is fun and there's nothing to worry about.

Breathe in and remember you always have plenty.
Breathe out and feel better than ever.

Gather all of your attention and focus it in this moment right here right now.

Breathe in and lift yourself up.
Breathe out and let this day be magickal.

You are divine! You get to choose to practice your magick today. How do you practice your magick? Just enter the present moment. If you like, you can think about what you want first, then enter the present moment. Your presence is your craft, and the more present you can be, the more the things you want will flock to you. In the present you are whole and you already have everything you need. When you're projecting a vibration of already having what you want, it has no choice but to come to you.

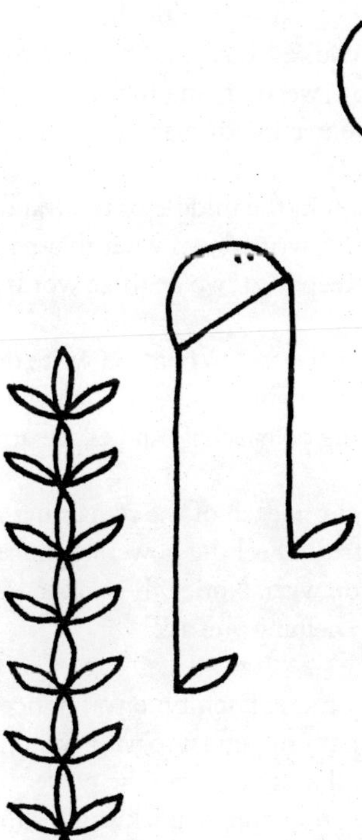

1

Magick Wand

Your pain is your power. Your pain is the energy that you transmute into gold. Your pain causes you to ask for what you truly want. And the universe is giving it to you. But if you are still pained by it, then you've become so distracted by the pain that you've forgotten how to align with well being on that topic. You've built up a lot of resistant thoughts around this topic.

But in the same way, you've launched a lot of desires. And every single one of those desires has been answered by the universe. So, in all of your asking, you've built up quite a bountiful treasure for yourself on the other side of the wave. Now, we are going to use your magick wand to help you align yourself with that side of the wave.

Write down what pains you in the middle of the wand. In one of the lines radiating from the wand, write down what that pain is causing you to ask for. Keep it to two or three words.

Do you believe your focus creates? When you write down the pivot thought, can you feel whether you believe it? Can you feel how your reality is reflecting your beliefs and expectations?

Write the same pivot thought in each of the remaining radiations. Each time you write it, feel its truth. Feel the power of your focus and your ability to direct it where you wish. Notice the blessing in your pain for helping you ask.

You don't have to suffer any more. Each time you notice yourself in this same old painful thought pattern, return to your wand. Remember the magick radiating from it and how you have the power to focus on what you prefer. The more you do, the more magick you'll allow into your life.

2

Sigil Magick

A sigil is a symbol of a magician's desired outcome. The most important aspect of creating your sigil is deciding upon your intent. You must figure out exactly what you want, and that can be a challenge. Be as specific as you can. Phrase your statement as an affirmation, such as:

I AM A MILLIONAIRE LIVING IN NYC.

1. Write your Statement of Intent.
(e.g., I am a millionaire living in NYC.)

2. Remove double letters and vowels.
(MLNRVGYC)

3. Simplify the letters into a symbol.

4. Draw and redraw the symbol until it becomes meaningless.

5. Draw your final symbol on a scrap of paper. Destroy it in a memorable manner. Send the signal to the universe that your statement of intent is now reality.

6. Forget your sigil completely. Be a cooperative component and take every lead that comes your way.

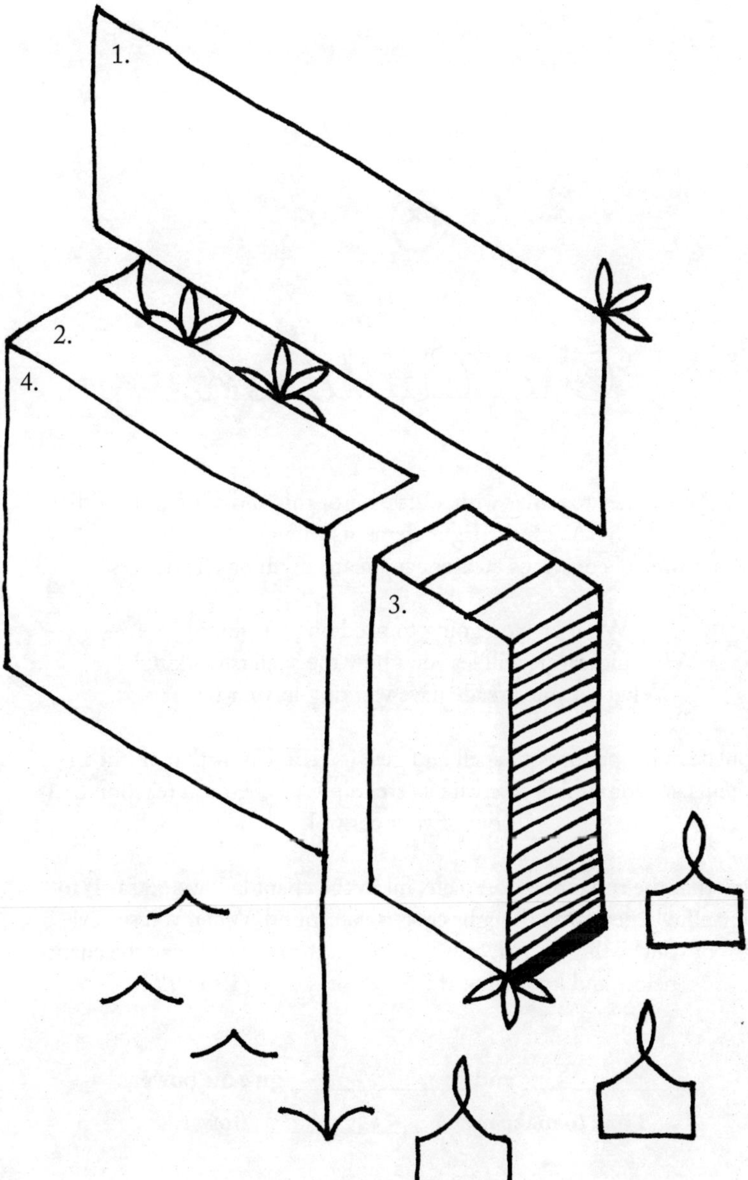
1.
2.
4.
3.

3

The Cauldron

Every spell comes together with a little bit of this and a little bit of that.
With the right elements though,
a powerful conscious creator can create anything she desires.

What are you going to need on your side?
What indicators will let you know the spell is working?
What do you already have working in your favor?

Concoct a recipe for your spell and give it a stir. Know that all the ingredients are combining to create a serendipitous chemical reaction that is out of your control.

Now that the mixture is complete, fill in the chant below and say it to yourself whenever the thought crosses your mind. When you see evidence of your spell working, or when you start to doubt it, say the chant below and know that the universe is doing its work.

______________ and ______________ give me power,
Time to make my ________________ flower.

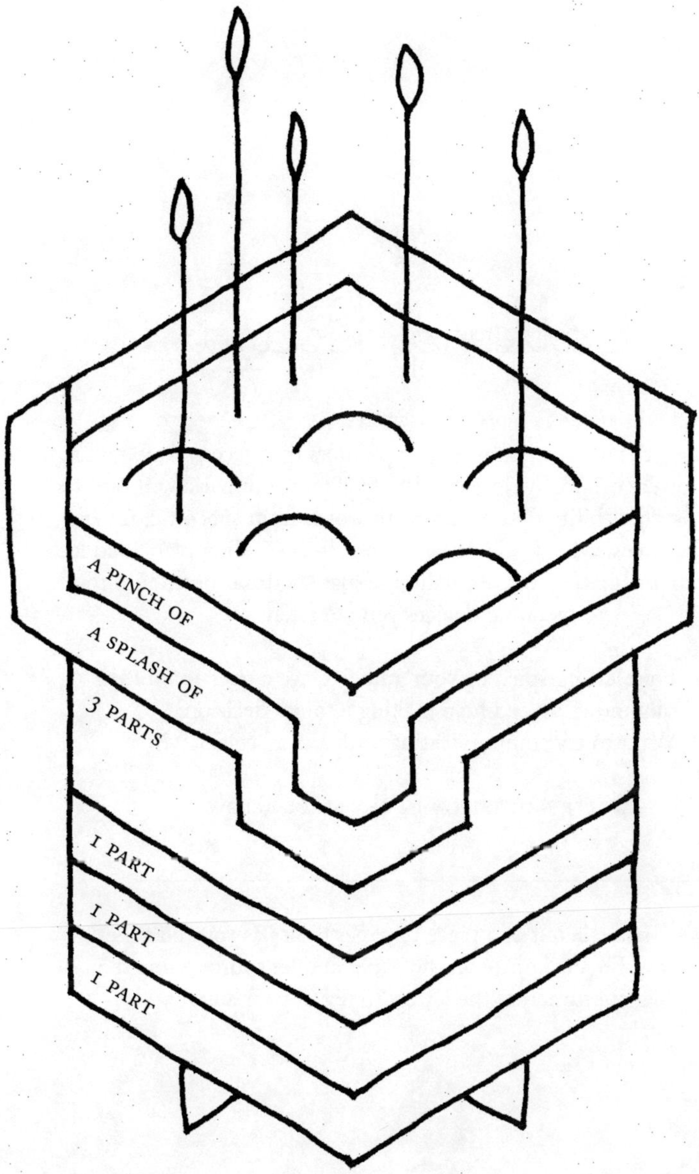

The purpose of this spell:

____

4

Talking Board

Planchettes, the usually heart-shaped pointers that accompany "talking boards", were originally developed to facilitate automatic writing—a type of psychic ability that brings forth words from subconscious and spiritual sources. One would place her pen in the rolling plank and let the mediumship begin. Eventually, the planchettes evolved into the dictating devices you see today.

How about letting spirit be your guide? Have a question for the unknown? Need help making a tough decision?
Want to try communicating with a dead celebrity?

WRITE A QUESTION IN THE SPACE BELOW

____

Now cut a triangle out of a piece of paper to use as your planchette. Place your fingers lightly on the paper and let source guide the planchette across the letters to reveal your answer.

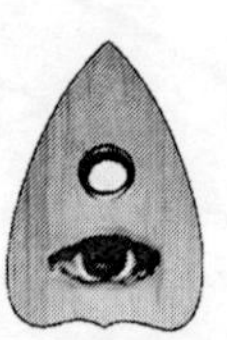

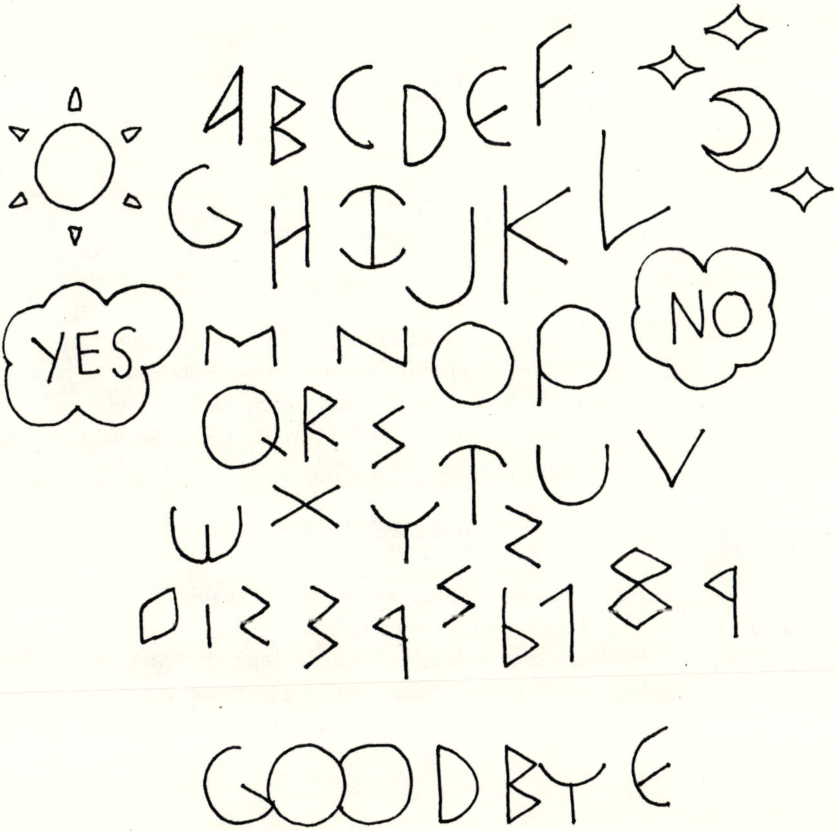
ABCDEF
GHIJKL
YES
MNOP
NO
QRS
TUV
WXYZ
0123456789
GOODBYE

5

Vision Board

Much like automatic writing, automatic drawing can reveal images from the subconscious or spirit mind. Take a moment to clear your mind and center yourself. Make a space for spirit to be pulled through you. Close your eyes and allow your hand to draw whatever it is moved to draw. Then open your eyes.

What do you see?

Unlike a traditional vision board which often involves the mind's version of what it thinks it wants, this vision board goes beyond the mind to paint a picture of your energy as it already stands. The energy you are choosing to project is the life image you are choosing to create. You may or may not like what it shows you, but it is always an accurate portrayal.

6

Talisman

Have you ever had a good luck charm? What made it so lucky? Was it the person who gave it to you? The circumstances under which you received it? Sentimental value?

No matter how the object became lucky, it was most likely deemed so by you. You have that power. You have the power to charge things with your energy. You have the power to decide that these symbols can have a positive (or negative) effect on your life.

Draw a good luck talisman in the crystal and decide what it will bring you. Consider the example magickal symbols below for inspiration. Try imbuing your own meanings on symbols such as: numbers, celestial bodies, tarot suits (cups, wands, pentacles, swords), shapes, characters, animals, or natural elements.

Eye fixity of purpose, poise, and stability
Fish abundance, prosperity
Frog health, fertility, long life
Ladder overcome & surmount difficulties in the material world

Keep the talisman you've made with you wherever you go, so you're reminded of the constant good fortune the universe is bestowing on you.

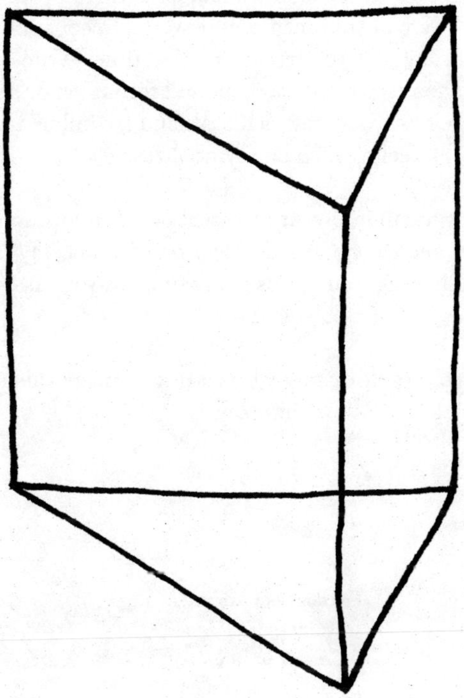

Ritual Altar

For each of the symbols on the altar, remember a time in your life when you were acutely aware of your magickal powers as a conscious creator. Remember specifically how you felt during that time. Write a keyword or words to help you recall that moment and feeling on or near each symbol. These are now your magickal tools and are imbued with the feeling each one symbolizes.

Any time you want to tap into your magickal power, return to your altar. Visit each symbol one by one. As you focus on each one, say the words and feel the feeling. Do you this as many times as you need to feel charged up.

Now go about your spell-casting with a sense of magickal knowing within you!

1. Freedom and Adventure
2. Clarity and Knowing
3. Creative or Intuitive
4. Love or Connection
5. Passion or Excitement
6. Power or Certainty
7. Flow
8. Accomplished
9. Abundant or Wealthy
10. Secure and Safe
11. Fearless and Strong

1.
2.
3.
4.
5.
6.
7.
8.
9.
10.
11.

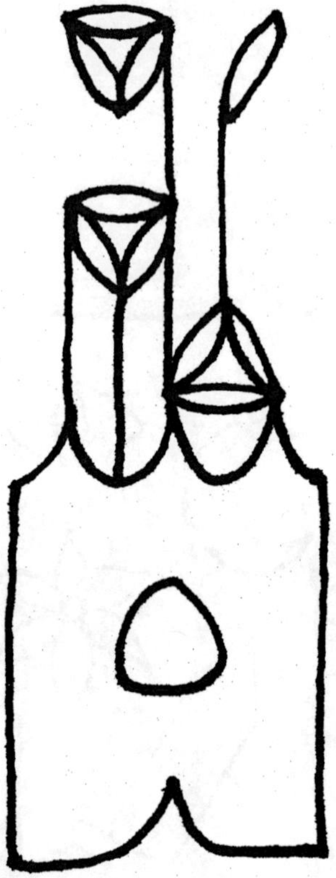